delicious diabetic recipes

Managing Diabetes

Table of Contents

Taking Control

You don't have to be a prisoner of diabetes. You can actively participate in your care, using the management tools at your disposal, in order to feel better and enjoy improved health and tighter diabetes control. In *Managing Diabetes*, we'll talk about lifestyle changes that you can take to help manage your diabetes: from foods to seek out to suggestions for getting active to tips for tracking your own care chart.

Much of the book offers information and strategy related to food. Eating is essential to life, but we eat for many reasons: out of hunger and habit, for pleasure, even as a way of dealing with emotions. A diagnosis of diabetes can make the simple act of eating seem overwhelmingly complicated. With education and experimentation, however, you can turn eating into a powerful diabetes management tool.

A Diabetic Diet?

When you learned you had diabetes, you may have assumed you'd have to go on a special, restrictive diet. Perhaps you'd heard of people with diabetes who had to give up every food they enjoyed or who stopped going to certain events or restaurants because there was nothing they could eat there. Well, cheer up. You don't need to follow a "diabetic diet" anymore.

A diet implies that you need to eat sparingly or accordingly to strict prescribed rules. Diets also have a nasty habit of prohibiting rich, high-calorie foods. Research shows that dieters often experience overwhelming cravings for foods they're not supposed to eat—and that they often give in. When they do, they frequently overindulge. The diet/binge cycle is very common in those who go on weight-loss diets. It leads to weight regain, yo-yo dieting, feelings of guilt, and constant food cravings.

Those who followed a traditional diabetic diet were no different than other dieters; they, too, would give in to their desires and binge on "forbidden" foods. When trying to totally avoid certain foods, people instead tend to overconsume them in the end. And for people with diabetes, the diet/binge cycle could lead not only to the usual consequences, but to poor diabetes control.

Rather than a restrictive diet, what you need is knowledge and information. You need to understand how food fuels and affects your body, especially your glucose levels, and then use that information, along with glucose monitoring, to choose a variety of foods—including the ones you enjoy most.

How Foods Affect Glucose

Your body needs adequate amounts of six essential nutrients to function normally. Three of these—water, vitamins, and minerals—provide no energy and do not affect blood glucose levels.

The other three—carbohydrate, protein, and fat—provide your body the energy it needs to work. This energy is measured in calories. Any food that contains calories will cause your blood glucose levels to rise. For your body to properly use these energy calories, it needs insulin.

Whenever you eat, your food is digested and broken down into your body's primary fuel source, glucose. While all energy nutrients are broken down into glucose, carbohydrates have a more direct effect on blood glucose levels. Protein and fat have a slower, more indirect effect. Understanding this can help you predict how food will affect your glucose levels.

Carbohydrates

Commonly known as sugars and starches, carbohydrates are your body's main, and preferred, source of energy. They enter your bloodstream rapidly, are fairly predictable in the way they affect glucose, and are generally broken down completely in about two hours.

There are three types: simple carbohydrates, or sugars (such as table sugar or honey); digestible complex carbohydrates, or starches (in bread, pasta, and potatoes); and nondigestible complex carbohydrates, or fiber.

Nearly 100 percent of the sugars and starches you eat break down into glucose; they do so at about the same speed, regardless of their source.

There are two types of simple carbohydrates, monosaccharides and disaccharides. Monosaccharides, such as glucose and fructose, are single sugar units. Disaccharides consist of two sugar units. For example, sucrose, or table sugar, is made of a glucose sugar hooked to a fructose sugar.

Digestible complex carbohydrates, or starches, are polysaccharides. They consist of many long chains of glucose units hooked together. Starches are found in grains, legumes, and potatoes. When starches are digested by your body, they are broken down into glucose, the simplest form of energy. The starch in your potato and the sugar in your sugar bowl, therefore, are really the same as far as your body is concerned. It has no way of knowing whether the energy originally came from a simple carbohydrate or a complex one.

However, people with diabetes often think, or have been taught, that they cannot have any simple carbohydrates, or sugar, in their diet. People assumed that simple carbohydrates were more quickly digested and absorbed into the blood than more complex starches, and that simple sugars would cause a large rise in blood glucose levels.

However, after several conclusive studies, the American Diabetes Association changed its nutritional recommendations. It is now generally recognized that the total amount of carbohydrate in your diet, not the source, is what significantly influences your blood glucose levels.

Proteins

The second major nutrient needed by your body is protein. The protein in the foods you eat (meats, poultry, fish, beans, dairy products, and eggs) is broken down by amino acids by your body. Only about 50 percent of it is eventually changed into glucose.

This is a long process, however. It takes about three to five hours after a meal for the protein you have eaten to have any impact on your blood glucose. When carbohydrates and fats are not available or are in short supply (as when you don't eat between your evening meal and breakfast the next morning), amino acids can be made into glucose as a back-up source of energy for the brain and other vital organs.

Fat

The third nutrient needed by your body is fat. Fat is used to maintain healthy skin and hair, to carry fat-soluble vitamins throughout your body, and as a major source of energy when you take in fewer calories than your body needs.

Fats are changed by your body into fatty acids, which are an important source of energy for your muscles and heart. It generally takes about six to eight hours for the fat in food to be digested, and its components are released very slowly into your blood. In the end, only about 5 to 10 percent of the fat you eat is changed into glucose, so it has little direct impact on your blood glucose levels.

Indirectly, however, fat does play a role in elevating blood glucose. Fat blocks the action of insulin and increases the time it takes for food to travel through your intestines. So if you eat a large dinner of fried chicken and mashed potatoes with gravy, it may not greatly affect your glucose reading before bed. During the night, however, when this fatty, slow-moving meal finally hits your system and the fat doesn't let your insulin work very well, your blood glucose level rises. In the morning, you awaken to a whopper of a blood glucose level.

Carbs Are Key

So now you have a basic understanding of how the nutrients in food affect your blood glucose. To use this knowledge successfully, you need to make personal food choices that are compatible with your blood glucose goals and your tastes. Since carbohydrates have the greatest direct effect on glucose levels, determining the amount of carbohydrates that your body can manage well is a cornerstone in your glucose management.

To gain a more detailed and concrete understanding of how you can use your food choices to control your blood sugar levels, you must pay attention to how individual foods act in your body. Approach this just as a scientist would, collecting data about blood glucose and types and amounts of foods, then drawing conclusions that are based on that data. Take detailed, honest notes on what you eat. Along with taking these notes, test your blood glucose levels. Testing will allow you to see how well your insulin level matches your carbohydrate level. Eat a variety of carbohydrates, proteins, and fats. Look for patterns in the ways various foods and food combinations affect your blood glucose level.

Learning to Choose

How, when, and what we eat and how we live can go a long way towards helping us improve our blood pressure, cholesterol levels, and glucose control, as well as shed some unwanted pounds. A healthier path than dieting is learning to choose. It's a path you can stay on for life. Unlike dieting, which is all about restrictions, learning to choose healthier foods and eating habits is all about expanding your dietary horizons. It's a skill that can bring joy and pleasure back into eating as you tackle diabetes. Below, you'll find some key strategies for eating well.

Know How Foods Affect Your Body

Check your glucose after meals to find out how different levels of carbohydrates affect your blood glucose levels. Be aware of how various types of fat affect blood cholesterol and how salt affects blood pressure. Use this information when you're shopping, along with food labels, to compare foods and make healthier choices.

Don't Label Foods as Good or Bad

No single food, in and of itself, is good or bad. A chocolate bar, a piece of prime rib, a slice of bread—not one of those is bad, nor does eating one of them mean you've failed somewhere.

Even though you have diabetes, each food can fit into your healthy eating plan, as long as you adjust for it. If enjoying it once in a while, in a reasonable portion, keeps you satisfied and out of the common trap of denying yourself foods and then binging on them, then it helps you out in the end.

Expand Your Food Options

Go ahead, dive into those grocery aisles and start experimenting! The more foods you try, the more likely you are to find a wide variety of tasty, desirable foods that match your body's nutrient needs and move you closer to your health goals. That doesn't mean you can't have your old favorites once in a while—but you'll also have some options lower in calories, fat, or sodium.

Say No to Quick Fixes

When you diet, there's an assumption that you will reach a certain goal—or give up—and go off the diet. Learning to choose isn't like that. Instead, each time you eat becomes an opportunity to choose something lower in salt or fat, something higher in fiber, or food that's richer in vitamins. You make the changes as you are able. Eventually, making healthier choices becomes the norm. Along the way, you discover you've dropped a few pounds, improved your control, and lowered your blood pressure and cholesterol.

When you learn to choose, the ball is in your court. It is up to you how often you make a healthier food choice, how quickly you move toward your goals, and exactly what a healthy, enjoyable diet consists of for you.

The ABCs of Eating Well for Insulin Users

Adjust when necessary. Eating the same portions at the same time every day makes it easier to maintain blood sugar control. Decide in advance if you want to splurge; if you take insulin, knowing how to adjust your dose can prevent blood sugar spikes.

Balance your diet. Eat a balanced diet that includes plenty of fruits, vegetables, beans, and whole grains.

Consistency is key. If you take insulin or insulin-promoting medication, eat at the same time every day. That makes it easier to time the medicine's onset with the rise of glucose levels in the blood. Avoid skipping meals.

A Varied Diet

As we've discussed, restricting yourself tends to backfire. Expand your food options instead—when you make your diet varied and tasty, it will be easier to make it healthy as well.

Take Advantage of Exchanges

To make it simple to add variety to meals, the American Dietetic Association and the American Diabetes Association publish easy-to-use exchange lists. Foods are grouped by categories, such as starches, vegetables, fruits, meats, and so on, with predetermined portion sizes. All food exchanges within a category have roughly equivalent nutritional levels and impact on blood sugar levels.

For instance, if you wake up some morning and decide you want a bowl of cereal or oatmeal instead of your usual toast, an exchange list can tell you how much cereal or oatmeal you can eat and still keep your blood sugar level in the target range. Ask your diabetes educator or dietitian about exchange lists. You'll also notice that the recipes in the cookbooks in this set will give you information about exchanges!

Get Colorful

One way to add variety to your diet is to add more foods with an array of different colors. Nutritionists believe that the same chemicals that give certain kinds of fruits and vegetables a brilliant hue may also promote health and fight disease. Tomatoes and watermelon, for example, get their red color from an antioxidant called lycopene, which may prevent some cancers.

You may want to see green on your plate, in particular. Some researchers believe that the antioxidants lutein and zeaxanthin, which are found in spinach, collards, kale, and broccoli, may strengthen the retina, the ring of nerve cells in the eyes that are vulnerable to blinding damage from high blood sugar.

Don't peel off the edible skin of apples or other fruits, either. That can strip away fiber and nutrients.

Managing Food Cravings

What about those times when you have a strong craving for a specific food, and nothing else will do? At one time or another, most of us have experienced an almost-irresistible urge to eat a certain food. These cravings are often less about fulfilling hunger and more about combating stress and easing anxiety.

Most commonly, we crave foods with a combination of carbohydrates (often sugar) and fat. We often crave foods that are not the most nutritious and are high in calories and fat. And we often crave foods that are easy to overeat, things like cookies and chips.

So how can you reduce food cravings? Here are some strategies you can try:

- Keep your hunger under control. Don't delay or skip meals. Eating regular meals can help control intense cravings for food that's easy to access, like candy bars, chips, and cookies.

- Get up and move. Craving will often subside while you're active.

- Drink a glass of water. Sometimes, cravings for food may be thirst in disguise.

- Train your taste buds. Over time, taste buds can get used to eating less sugar, fat, and salt. Be patient, as this can take time. Slowly cutting back is more realistic and sustainable than trying to abstain altogether.

- Try smart carbs. Foods like whole grains, fruits, and vegetables provide the carbs along with nutritional power. Combine these with protein foods like nuts, cheese, or yogurt to satisfy your taste buds and keep your blood sugar levels more even.

- Sometimes, allow yourself to surrender. Let yourself have a small portion of the food you're craving. A few bites may be all you need to fulfill your craving and get it off your mind.

Trimming Down on Fat

The connection may not seem obvious, but if you have diabetes, you need to be concerned about your heart. People with diabetes are three times more likely to develop heart disease. So as you learn to choose healthier foods, it's important to keep your blood cholesterol level and your risk of heart disease in mind—and in check. Cutting down the fat in your diet can help, especially cutting out saturated and trans fats. It can also help improve your blood glucose control, since fat can indirectly elevate your blood glucose levels by blocking the action of insulin.

Is Fat Bad?

Of course not! Fat provides energy, and we need some fat to absorb the fat-soluble vitamins A, D, E, and K. And no one can deny that fat adds flavor and juiciness to food. It's just that we tend to eat more of it than our bodies can handle in a healthy manner. Also, many processed foods that we eat tend to be higher in the fats that can raise cholesterol and damage arteries.

Making Choices

As you cut down on fat, you can use these two strategies: choosing more foods that have less total fat and substituting healthier fats for some of the saturated ones you normally eat. See the table on the next page for a breakdown of foods and their fat content. Here are some tips for making your choices:

- Read food labels and opt more often for food with less total fat and less saturated fat.
- Use fat-free and low-fat milk products.

- Eat a variety of fruits and vegetables, whole-grain products, beans, and nuts. Fruits and vegetables are naturally low in fat and provide loads of nutrients. Whole-grain foods and beans are low in fat but high in nutrients. Nuts, while not especially low in fat, are filled with mostly monounsaturated fats.
- Choose fish more often than poultry; choose poultry more often than red meat.
- Trim visible fat from meat and fat and skin from poultry before eating.
- Instead of frying, try baking, broiling, roasting, or grilling.
- Choose fats and oils that are trans-fat free and have two grams or less of saturated fat per tablespoon.

The Types of Fat

Saturated, monounsaturated, and polyunsaturated are the three main types of fat. The more saturated a fat is, the more detrimental it can be when eaten to excess.

What It Is	What It Does	Where It's Found
Saturated fats	These fats lead to more LDL molecules, the "bad" type of cholesterol.	Red meat, poultry, cheese, butter, full-fat dairy products; palm, coconut, and palm kernel oils
Trans fats	Trans fats are created when unsaturated fats are "resaturated." This makes them act more like saturated fats in the body; they tend to raise total blood cholesterol. The use of trans fats is regulated in some cities and states.	Many breads, crackers, cookies, doughnuts, frozen pie crusts, deep-fried foods, fast foods, packaged and convenient foods
Monounsaturated fats	These fats lower the number of LDL molecules.	Olive, canola, and peanut oils; olives; avocados; most nuts, including almonds, cashews, and pecans; peanuts and natural peanut butter
Polyunsaturated fats	These can be divided into two types. *Omega 6 fatty acids* can cause water retention, raise blood pressure, increase blood clotting, and decrease "good" HDL cholesterol. *Omega 3 fatty acids* can lower blood cholesterol and heart disease risk by making blood less likely to clot	Omega 6: Corn, cottonseed, sunflower, and soybean oils; **many** processed foods. Omega 3: Many fish, including wild salmon, mackerel, sardines, herring, anchovies, rainbow trout, bluefish, caviar, white albacore tuna; canola oil; flaxseed and flaxseed oil; walnuts and walnut oil; and dark green, leafy vegetables

Managing Your Salt Intake

Salt isn't bad—it contains sodium, an essential mineral for the human body. However, too much sodium contributes to high blood pressure, which is especially common to and dangerous for people with type 2 diabetes. Decreasing your salt intake can help reduce your blood pressure, which cuts down on your risk of heart attack, stroke, and kidney problems.

By the Numbers

Normal minimum sodium requirement: 400 milligrams (mg) a day—about one-fifth of a teaspoon of table salt

Maximum recommended level: 1,500 mg a day

Tips for Reducing Your Sodium Intake

- Be aware: Read food labels. Processed foods can contain a lot more sodium than you expect. They account for most of the salt and sodium you consume each day.

- When the option is available, choose no-salt-added or reduced-sodium products.

- Buy fresh produce. There's no salt added.

- Use fresh poultry, fish, and lean meats more often than canned, smoked, or processed types.

- Use low-sodium versions of soy sauce and teriyaki sauce.

- Use herbs, spices, lemon, lime, vinegar, or salt-free seasoning blends. Start by replacing half of the salt you would normally use.

- Use brown rice, whole-grain pasta, and whole-grain hot cereals cooked without salt.

- Take the salt shaker off the table.
- Always taste your food before adding any salt.
- When eating foods that are pickled, cured, in broth, or bathed in soy sauce, choose only small portions.
- When dining out, ask that your food be prepared without added salt, monosodium glutamate (MSG), or high-sodium ingredients.
- Limit salty condiments such as ketchup, mustard, pickles, and mayonnaise. Experiment: Try at least one bite of your food without condiments. If you do add them on, add just enough to get a hint of their taste. Eat foods that you only enjoy with condiments sparingly.

Bringing Down Your Blood Pressure

Reducing your sodium intake isn't the only dietary change that can help bring down your blood pressure. Plan meals that are:

- Low in saturated fat, cholesterol, red meat, and simple carbohydrates
- Rich in fruits, vegetables, low-fat dairy foods, whole-grain products, fish, poultry, and nuts
- Rich in magnesium (found in nuts, seeds, dried beans, and bananas), potassium, and calcium

Sodium Surprises

Minimal Sodium	Low Sodium	Moderate Sodium	High Sodium
olive oil, 1 tbsp = 0 mg	unsalted butter, 1 tbsp = 2 mg	butter, salted, 1 tbsp = 116 mg	margarine, 1 tbsp = 140 mg
fresh corn, 1 ear = 1 mg	frozen corn, 1 cup = 7 mg	corn flakes, 1 cup = 256 mg	canned corn, 1 cup = 384 mg
cucumber, 7 slices = 2 mg	sweet pickle, 1 = 128 mg	cucumber w/ salad dressing = 234 mg	dill pickle, 1 = 928 mg
lemon, 1 = 1 mg	catsup, 1 tbsp = 156 mg	soy sauce, 1 tbsp = 1,029 mg	salt, 1 tbsp = 1,938 mg
potato, 1 = 5 mg	potato chips, 10 chips = 200 mg	mashed potatoes, instant, 1 cup = 485 mg	potato salad, ½ cup = 625 mg
tuna, fresh, 3 oz = 50 mg	tuna, canned, 3 oz = 384 mg	tuna pot pie, 1 frozen = 715 mg	fish sandwich, 1 fast-food = 882 mg
peanuts, unsalted, 1 cup = 8 mg	peanut butter, 1 tbsp = 81 mg	peanut brittle, 1 oz = 145 mg	dry roasted peanuts, salted, 1 cup = 986 mg

The Scoop on Fiber

Back in the 1980s, there was a period when oat bran bread became the toast of the town. Research suggested that eating oats and other high-fiber foods could fight heart disease and some cancers. Boring bran cereal became hip, and consumers switched from white bread to dark loaves.

Since food trends come and go, fiber's reputation as a health savior has faded slightly. And while fiber can improve blood glucose levels, research shows that it would do so when used in very, very large amounts—about four to five times the amount that people usually eat!

However, there are health benefits—for example, eating foods with soluble fiber can help improve blood cholesterol levels—so there's no doubt that fiber should play an important role in any heart-healthy diet.

What's more, foods that are high in fiber can help you feel fuller longer on fewer calories and without increasing your blood sugar. Fat can fill you up as well—but fat has almost twice as many calories per gram as high-fiber foods.

Two Kinds of Fiber

Fiber is made up mostly of complex carbohydrates—so complex, in fact, that they cannot be broken down by enzymes in your body. There are two kinds of fiber in food:

Insoluble fiber: This is fibrous stuff in plants that doesn't dissolve as it passes through the gastrointestinal system, so you can't digest it. Instead, it absorbs water and helps move waste through the colon. Insoluble fiber delays glucose absorption and slows the breakdown of starch, but it increases the speed at which food moves through your intestines.

Soluble fiber: Soluble fiber isn't digested either, but in your gut, it grabs fat molecules before they can be absorbed into the blood, whisking them out of the body through the intestines. Soluble fiber delays glucose absorption and lowers cholesterol. It decreases the speed at which food moves through your intestines.

Sources of Insoluble Fiber

- Grapes/Raisins
- Broccoli
- Legumes
- Seeds
- Whole-wheat bread
- Whole grains
- Zucchini
- Cabbage
- Barley
- Dark leafy vegetables

Sources of Soluble Fiber

- Pears
- Dried peas and beans
- Carrots
- Cereals
- Apples
- Lentils
- Oat bran and oatmeal
- Cucumbers
- Oranges
- Celery

What about Fiber Supplements?

Fiber supplements can offer a convenient and effective way to add bulk to your diet, but try to get your fill from foods instead. High-fiber pills, powders, and snacks contain natural substances such as psyllium seed husks (which come from a type of plaintain). But fiber-dense foods are also excellent sources of vitamins, minerals, and other healthy stuff. What's more, fiber supplements are commonly used as laxatives, so it's important to use them as—and only when—prescribed.

Adding Fiber Slowly

If you are planning to add fiber to your diet, start slowly to avoid developing flatulence. While insoluble fiber passes through the gut with little fanfare, soluble fiber is attached by enzymes in the large intestine. The process produces a variety of gasses, which can cause abdominal discomfort—and social embarrassment.

Doctors recommend increasing fiber intake by a small amount each week to allow your body time to adjust to your new diet. Over-the-counter products may help reduce gassiness, and drinking plenty of fluids will help prevent constipation.

Food FAQs

On these pages, we'll look at some popular foods and food trends to help you decide what's right for you.

Is a gluten-free diet good for people with diabetes?

Gluten-free foods have become more popular over the last few years. If you have celiac disease in addition to diabetes, talk with your diabetic care team about a gluten-free diet. However, those without celiac disease will not receive benefits from following a gluten-free diet. It will not improve your blood glucose levels.

Are coffee, tea, and soda okay to drink?

Coffee and tea are fine to drink, as long as you're able to tolerate caffeine. However, in persons with diabetes, drinking caffeinated coffee has been shown to have beneficial effects, such as decreasing insulin resistance and lowering levels of artery inflammation.

For those who crave soda, stick to diet soft drinks and avoid sugar-sweetened soda. Use moderation in drinking diet soft drinks.

Should I cut out red meat altogether?

Beef has a bad reputation, but it does have health benefits. It provides good protein and essential vitamins and minerals, including easily-absorbed iron.

Cutting out beef is unnecessary for most people. It can even be unhealthy, since allowing yourself to enjoy lean beef offers variety that may help you stick with a heart-healthy diet in the long run. Choose cuts of lean beef, keep your portions moderate, and use a low-fat cooking method such as roasting, broiling, grilling, stir-frying, braising, or stewing.

Do people with diabetes need to give up chocolate?

If you were worried that you might have to give up chocolate altogether, set those fears aside! In fact, chocolate contains some antioxidants that can provide health benefits, reducing both blood pressure and LDL (bad) cholesterol. The antioxidants are strongest in cocoa powder, then in dark chocolate, then in milk chocolate. So when you're shopping, look for dark chocolate with a high cocoa content, and enjoy it in moderation—an ounce of dark chocolate once or twice a week.

Can I follow a vegetarian or vegan diet? Should I?

People with diabetes can definitely follow a vegetarian or vegan diet if they'd like to. And any person with diabetes who is trying to expand their food options may want to incorporate more vegetarian meals in their eating plan. It's most important to find a way of eating that you can sustain over time. Carbohydrate counting, simplified meal plans, healthy food choices, and reducing calories and fat have all been shown to improve blood glucose levels.

Which oils are best to use?

One thing to remember is that all oils are pure fat, so use oils sparingly. However, it's also important to remember that some oils are healthier than others. Your best bet is to choose a variety of oils, using them judiciously. Canola oil, olive oil, and nut oils are all rich in monounsaturated fat. Canola oil's mild taste makes it a good all-purpose cooking oil. Olive oil may help lower blood cholesterol levels; look for extra-virgin olive oil, which is the least processed and most flavorful type. Soybean oil supplies a fair amount of omega-3 fatty acids, and its mild flavor makes it good for baking.

In the Spotlight

On these pages, we'll focus the spotlight on some specific foods you just might want to include in your varied diet!

Benefit from Beans

Lowly legumes are among the healthiest foods on the planet. They're packed with fiber, protein, B vitamins, and other nutrients. Try an array of beans, from garbanzos to great northern.

Fantastic Figs

Figs are a nutrition powerhouse. In addition to having more potassium, fiber, and calcium than any other fruit, they also contain disease-fighting antioxidants. The potassium in figs helps to control blood pressure—since people with diabetes are at a higher risk for hypertension, figs are a smart snack.

Go with the (Whole) Grain

Most Americans grew up eating white bread, white pasta, and white rice. The process used to refine wheat or rice removes some valuable nutrients. Whole-grain breads, pasta, and rice are made with the entire grain, preserving valuable nutrients. Often, whole grains have a bolder taste and chewier texture than their paler cousins. Add them to your diet, and over time, you may find that white bread and other refined grains taste bland. Be careful and make sure that the packaging says "whole grain" or "whole wheat," as some commercial bakeries sell "wheat" bread that is simply white bread dyed brown.

Great Greens

Cooked greens, such as collard greens, dandelion greens, mustard greens, turnip greens, Swiss chard, and kale are a perfect side dish for many meals. They are hearty, flavorful, and packed with nutrients, especially vitamin A, vitamin C, iron, and calcium.

Outstanding Olives

Olives are packed with heart-healthy compounds, most notably monounsaturated fats. In addition, recent studies have shown that the fat found in olives and olive oil can help to lower blood pressure. Finally, the high antioxidant content of olives protects and benefits the cardiovascular system, respiratory system, nervous system, musculoskeletal system, immune system, and digestive system.

Sensational Sweet Potatoes

Their name may contain the word "sweet," but these root vegetables aren't high in sugar. They're extremely nutrient-rich and are often ranked as one of the healthiest foods. They're great for people with diabetes; they're rich in nutrients including fiber, potassium, and magnesium, and in antioxidants such as beta-carotene and vitamin C. Their high potassium content helps maintain normal blood pressure. They have lots of vitamin A, which helps keep your eyes healthy.

Valuable Vinegar

If you're looking for a sharp burst of flavor to add to your meals, reach for the vinegar. Research shows that consuming 1 to 2 teaspoons of vinegar may lower post-meal blood sugar levels and increase feelings of fullness. Most vinegars have an insignificant amount of calories, but as always, check the nutrition label to be certain. Seasoned vinegars may provide more flavor, but they may also contain more calories.

Wonderful Walnuts

Go nuts over walnuts! Walnuts are one of the most nutritious nuts around, due to their combination of monounsaturated fats, omega-3 fatty acids, antioxidants, and fiber. A handful of walnuts makes a great heart-healthy snack.

Sweeteners and You

There are two types of sweeteners on the market today, those with calories, called nutritive sweeteners, and those with no calories, called artificial, or nonnutritive, sweeteners. Only the nutritive sweeteners affect blood glucose directly, but you'll still need to note the other ingredients in foods that use artificial sweeteners.

Nutritive Sweeteners

The simple carbohydrates sucrose and fructose are the most common nutritive sweeteners used. Both contribute calories and influence your blood glucose levels.

Sugar alcohols are often used as substitute sweeteners, especially in candy. Sugar alcohols can occur naturally in plants such as fruits and berries. However, the term also refers to the commercially produced, processed liquids from sucrose, glucose, and starches.

Sugar alcohols are not completely absorbed by your body, so they contribute fewer calories and carbohydrates than other nutritive sweeteners. However, they can produce unpleasant side effects, such as diarrhea, gas, and bloating, when consumed in excess.

Artificial Sweeteners

Artificial sweeteners are man-made, intensely sweet products. They're most commonly used in reduced-calorie foods and beverages. They add very few, if any, calories and carbohydrates to food.

"Sugar-Free" Products

When it comes to the label "sugar free," it's important to read the fine print. If a product is labeled "sugar free," it only means that the product contains less than .5 grams of sucrose (table sugar or cane sugar). Manufacturers can add fructose and other nutritive sweeteners and still call their product "sugar free."

That means that in some cases, a "sugar-free" product can actually contain more total carbohydrates than the regular version of the same product. So always check the nutrition label and the list of ingredients, not just the label on the front of the box!

Nutritive sweeteners (contain calories)	
sucrose (white sugar)	It is very versatile in terms of use, readily available, and inexpensive.
glucose	It is mainly used in candies to provide smoothness at high temperatures. It has a lower level of sweetness than sucrose.
fructose	It enhances fruit flavors.
honey	It is nutritionally similar to sucrose. It has a distinctive flavor and a high water content.
lactose	This is the sugar found in milk. It has a low sweetness level, but it is often used in combination with intense sweeteners as a "filler." People who are lactose intolerant lack the digestive enzyme that helps break this sugar down.
sorbitol, mannitol	These sugar alcohols are about half as sweet as sucrose. They are incompletely absorbed by your body, and can cause digestive side effects when used in large quantities. They are more expensive than sucrose.
xylitol, maltitol	These sugar alcohols are widely used, especially in candies and baked goods. They are about as sweet as sucrose. They are incompletely absorbed by the body, and can cause digestive side effects when used in large quantities.
hydrogenated starch hydrolysate	It is widely used in candies and with low-calorie, nonnutritive sweeteners.
Nonnutritive sweeteners (calorie-free)	
saccharin (Sweet'N Low)	It provides no energy. This heat-stable sweetener can be used in cooking or baking. Though hundreds of times sweeter than sucrose, it can have a bitter aftertaste.
aspartame (NutraSweet, Equal)	While approved as a general purpose sweetener, it isn't heat stable for cooking or baking. It cannot be used by people with phenylketonuria.
acesulframe K (Sweet One)	This organic salt is 200 times sweeter than sucrose. It is heat stable.
sucralose (Splenda)	This sweetener is derived from sugar but is not digested. It is heat stable.
stevia (PureVia, Truvia)	It is derived from the purified leaves of a South American plant. It can be used for cooking and baking.

Alcohol and Diabetes

We usually categorize food and drink into carbohydrates, proteins, or fats, and they all provide energy. Where does alcohol fit in? It's not an energy source; in fact, the body treats it more as a toxin. Your body wants to break down, detoxify, and remove alcohol from your blood as quickly as possible to prevent it from accumulating and destroying cells and organs.

When you drink, alcohol passes very quickly from your stomach and intestines into your blood without being broken down. Enzymes in your liver then break down the alcohol, but this process takes time. Your liver can only metabolize alcohol at a set rate, regardless of how much you have had to drink. If you drink alcohol faster than it can be broken down, it moves through your bloodstream to other parts of your body until it can be metabolized. Your brain cells are affected by this excess, impairing brain function and causing intoxication.

Whether you have eaten and what you have eaten are two factors that influence how quickly alcohol is absorbed into your blood. Slowing down the absorption time can be beneficial. Studies show that eating after a meal that includes fat, protein, and carbohydrate helps you absorb alcohol more slowly than drinking on an empty stomach.

Alcohol and Glucose

When alcohol is in your system, the process of breaking it down cuts ahead of other processes on the liver's agenda. Normally, when your blood glucose level starts to drop, your liver responds by changing stored energy into glucose. But your liver will not make or release any glucose until the alcohol is gone from your system. That puts you at risk for a number of different problems, including a hypoglycemic reaction. Because alcohol can impair judgment, you may not even realize that you're having symptoms of hypoglycemia.

Is Drinking Alcohol Okay?

So what does all that mean? If you have diabetes, should you abstain from alcohol altogether, or can you have a beer with your pizza or a glass of wine with your spaghetti?

There is no one right answer. Whether you can drink is something that you should discuss with your diabetes care team, because it depends on your diabetes control, the medications you're taking, and your alcohol consumption. For those who can drink, here are a few guidelines:

1. Drink only if your diabetes is under good control, if you do not have frequent issues with hypoglycemia or a past history of severe hypoglycemia.

2. Drink in moderation. Moderation generally means no more than two drinks per day for men and no more than one per day for women. A single drink is defined as 12 ounces of beer, 5 ounces of wine, or 1 ½ ounces of distilled liquor.

3. Do not skip a meal or decrease food intake when drinking. Have your drink with a meal or shortly after eating. Never drink on an empty stomach.

4. Carry a form of identification that indicates that you have diabetes. If something goes wrong, this lets people know that erratic behavior or loss of consciousness may be due to severe hypoglycemia instead of intoxication.

5. Never drink alone. The people you're drinking with should know the signs and symptoms of hypoglycemia.

6. Remain sober. Don't compromise your need to eat your meals, take your medication, and test your blood sugar on schedule.

7. Test your blood glucose frequently. Test prior to drinking, after drinking, and the next day. Always test before going to sleep, but never give yourself extra insulin or take extra diabetes pills to treat a high blood glucose reading just before going to bed. You could become dangerously hypoglycemic as you sleep and never even notice.

Keeping Fit

The three cornerstones in the treatment of diabetes are food, medications, and activity. Moving toward a physically active life is generally inexpensive, convenient, and easy. It produces great rewards in terms of blood glucose control and a general feeling of well-being.

When you actively use a muscle, you burn both fatty acids and glucose. During and after periods of activity, your falling glucose level is sensed by the beta cells in your pancreas, and they relax their output of insulin. This gives your pancreas a break from excessive insulin production. In addition, the lower insulin levels signal your liver to empty its glucose reserves into the blood to supply the muscles with needed energy.

As physical activity continues, the liver converts amino acids, lactic acid, and fats into glucose to supply the muscles. If the activity continues long enough, even the body's fat cells get into the game. They compensate for the reduced fatty acid levels in your blood by converting their stored triglycerides into fatty acids. Overall, using your muscles helps you lower blood glucose, lower fatty acids levels in your blood, and reduce the workload of your pancreas.

Managing Risks

As well as the benefits, exercise does carry some risks for people with diabetes. For those who take medication or insulin, hypoglycemia is a concern. The march of glucose from the blood into the muscles doesn't end when activity stops, so a hypoglycemic reaction can occur not only during periods of activity but up to 24 hours later.

Some people with diabetes who have frequently experienced hypoglycemia begin to associate any form of activity with a loss of glucose control. Fluctuations in blood sugar create confusion and frustration, leaving people upset and scared. However, more frequent blood glucose testing can help people with diabetes better understand their body's response to exercise and prepare for it by adjusting medication or food intake.

People with diabetes also may have health complications. For example, coronary heart disease is very common in people with diabetes. Before you begin increasing your level of activity, consult your doctor and, if appropriate, have an exercise tolerance test. This test is done on a treadmill and reflects your heart's ability to work under stress. Even if you do have heart disease, you will likely still be able to increase your physical activity; you will just need to work more closely with your diabetes care team to set safe guidelines.

> ## Benefits of Being More Active
>
> - Lower blood glucose
> - Lower blood pressure
> - Lower blood fats
> - Better cardiovascular (heart and lung) fitness
> - Weight loss and/or maintenance
> - Improved sense of well-being

In addition, some types of activity may not be wise for people with certain medical conditions that are more common in people with diabetes. Any activity that involves straining, such as weight lifting, can dramatically increase blood pressure during the actual activity, further aggravating any hypertension that is present. You need to have your blood pressure well controlled before you start increasing your activity and especially before beginning an activity that involves straining.

Proliferative retinopathy is also aggravated by straining, which increases the pressure within some of the weakened blood vessels of the eyes. Activities that require straining or that involving jarring or rapid head motions may also cause an acute hemorrhage in weakened eye muscles. Before you begin an exercise program, have your eyes examined, and have them rechecked annually.

For those with nerve damage in their feet, take care to observe good foot care at home, inspecting your feet for sore spots and minor injuries daily. You'll also want to get your feet checked by your doctor first, get expert advice on proper footwear for the activity you're interested in, and be sure the footwear you choose is fitted properly.

Guidelines for Activity

- **See your physician** for a complete medical exam before adopting a new workout regimen.

- Choose activities that **fit your physical condition, lifestyle, and tastes.** Many people who have not been physically active for a while find that easy, low-impact activities such as walking and swimming are perfect.

- Make sure that whatever activities you choose are **enjoyable for you.** That increases the likelihood that you'll stick with them.

- **Vary your activities** so you don't get bored and fall prey to excuses. Choose some activities that can be done indoors in case of bad weather. Choose some activities that can be fit into a busy schedule.

- **Don't skimp** on exercise gear and equipment. Good-quality equipment pays for itself in the form of better protection against injuries. That's especially true for footwear. And always wear socks to keep your feet dry.

- **Warm up and cool down.** Always begin each exercise session with a five- to ten-minute period of low-intensity activity and gentle stretching. This prepares your heart for increased activity. It also give your muscles and joints a little time to get warm and loose. End your workouts with ten minutes of cool-down and more gentle stretching.

- Increase the amount of physical activity you do and its intensity slowly and **build up gradually**.

- Stay hydrated. **Drink plenty of water** before, during, and after exercise. Dehydration can spoil a good workout.

- **Identify yourself.** Just to be on the safe side, always wear a bracelet or shoe tag identifying yourself as a person with diabetes when you work out.

- Exercise at a level of **moderate intensity.** One way to determine this is to work with your care team to figure out your target heart range during exercise. You can also use the talk test: If you're breathing hard but can keep up a casual conversation while exercising, you're probably in the right range.

Staying active doesn't mean you need to "exercise" in the traditional sense, as long as you're moving. Square dancing, taking your dog on long walks, riding your bike, gardening, and even walking the golf course all count.

Avoiding Glucose Problems

To preempt problems with your glucose levels during and after exercise, there are a number of things you can do.

- Plan your activity to follow a meal so that it can help lower the increased blood glucose level that follows eating.

- Check your blood glucose 30 minutes before and just prior to activity. This way you can see which direction your glucose level is heading and anticipate a low in time to take preventive action.

- Plan for a possible hypoglycemic episode. Carry glucose tablets with you.

- If you manage diabetes with insulin, know the peak time of your insulin and plan your activities accordingly.

- When injecting insulin, avoid the muscle areas that you will be using during the activity. For example, if you will be playing tennis, avoid using your racket arm. Most people find the abdomen or buttocks work best before exercise.

- If your blood glucose level before activity is more than 250 mg/dl, check your urine for ketones. An elevated glucose level and positive ketones indicate that your diabetes is uncontrolled and that you need to contact your diabetes care team for advice immediately.

- Monitor your glucose during exercise to see what effect activity has on you. Check it every half hour during exercise and again when you are finished.

- If, during any activity, you experience shortness of breath, chest pain, or leg cramps that go away with rest, contact your doctor immediately. These are all possible signs of blocked arteries and require an evaluation by your doctor.

Chart Your Own Course

The latest approach to diabetes treatment puts you in charge. You become the boss of your diabetes team, choosing the staff that best serves your needs, tracking your progress, and keeping your eyes on the ultimate goal—your health and well-being.

Managing your diabetes is easier with a good team on board: knowledgeable, trustworthy, expert advisors who can give you information, advice, treatment, and support. Your team may include doctors (including an eye doctor, podiatrist, and cardiologist), a mental-health professional, a diabetes educator, a dietitian, a pharmacist, and a dentist. But because nobody knows your life better than you do, you are the general and boss of your team.

It is important that you and the members of your team develop a good working relationship where there is mutual understanding, respect, and trust. You will need to feel comfortable talking with and asking questions of your team members. If you are unable to develop such a relationship with one of your team members, you need to find someone else. Always remember that these people work for you.

One strategy for managing your diabetes is to keep your own care chart. This way, you have all your information about your diabetes in one place, and you can take it with you when you meet with another member of your care team. Especially if you see more than one doctor, they should know what medications that you have been prescribed or are taking over-the-counter so that dangerous interactions can be avoided.